CATCHING THE FIRE
Philip Simmons, Blacksmith

CATCHING THE FIRE
Philip Simmons, Blacksmith

Mary E. Lyons

With photographs by Mannie Garcia

Houghton Mifflin Company   Boston 1997

To Rossie Colter

Half-title page: Philip Simmons forged the stair rail, newel post, porch rail, and three sets of window grilles at 45 Meeting Street, Charleston, South Carolina.
Facing title page: Philip Simmons forges a wiggle tail in the early 1970s.
Title page: Students from Buist Academy on Visitor's Center Gate, Charleston, South Carolina.

Photo Credits
Pages 16, 43, facing title, and front cover: Philip Simmons Foundation, Charleston, South Carolina; John Michael Vlach, photographer
Pages 6, 14, 15, 23, 24, 29, 31, 33, 37, 38, 39, 45, 46, half-title, title, and back cover: Philip Simmons Foundation, Charleston, South Carolina; Mannie Garcia, photographer
Pages 10, 18, 20, 40: Philip Simmons Foundation, Charleston, South Carolina
Page 12: The South Carolina Historical Society, Charleston, South Carolina
Pages 25, 27, 32, 35: Courtesy of the author
Page 42: Museum of American History, Smithsonian Institution

For information about this and other Houghton Mifflin trade and reference books and multimedia products, visit The Bookstore at Houghton Mifflin on the World Wide Web at http://www.hmco.com/trade/.

The text of this book is set in 13.75 Monotype Dante.
Designed by S. M. Sherman, Ars Agassiz, Cambridge, Massachusetts.

Library of Congress Cataloging-in-Publication Data

Lyons, Mary E.
Catching the fire: Philip Simmons, blacksmith / by Mary E. Lyons.
p. cm.
Summary: Tells the story of this African-American artist, the great-grandson of slaves, who has achieved fame and admiration for his ornamental wrought-iron creations.
ISBN 0-395-72033-8
1. Simmons, Philip, 1912– — Juvenile literature. 2. Blacksmiths — South Carolina — Charleston — Biography — Juvenile literature. 3. Afro-Americans — South Carolina — Charleston — Biography — Juvenile literature. 4. Architectural ironwork — South Carolina — Charleston — Juvenile literature. [1. Simmons, Philip, 1912– . 2. Blacksmiths. 3. Afro-Americans — Biography.] I. Garcia, Mannie, ill. II. Title.
NA8392.S57L96 1997
739.4′72 — dc20
[B] 96-38643 CIP AC

Printed in Singapore
TWP 10 9 8 7 6 5 4 3 2 1

Contents

Detail of Snake Gate, 329 East Bay Street, Charleston, South Carolina

Introduction

Philip Simmons caught the blacksmith fever when he was thirteen years old. Since then the artist has forged more than five hundred pieces of ornamental wrought iron. Most of his gates, fences, and railings decorate the coastal city of Charleston, South Carolina. Several of his finest works are in museums.

To touch a Philip Simmons gate is to touch the past. His craft is over five thousand years old. In 3500 B.C., Egyptian smiths shaped metal with hammer and fire. In Sierra Leone, West Africa, smiths have worked brass and copper since the thirteenth century.

From 1670 until 1863, thousands of West Africans were enslaved on the coast of South Carolina. Some were blacksmiths who passed the tradition on to their offspring. One descendant, a former slave, showed Philip Simmons how to work iron.

Like his ancestors, Mr. Simmons can hammer life into a dead lump of iron. But he is the first African-American smith known to forge animal figures. His fish and sly-eyed snakes look as lively as he feels. "I like action!" he declares in his musical Low Country speech.

For over eighty years, action has guided Philip Simmons's life and art. Born on June 9, 1912, he claims he retired in 1987. Yet he remains excited about his craft. After a lifetime of seventeen-hour workdays, he still rises at six A.M.

Mr. Simmons often wakes with an idea for a new gate. "I see it finished completely in my mind," he says. Before breakfast, he rolls a squeaky chair up to his office desk and sketches the design.

And he will still play "the old blacksmith tune" on his anvil, especially for young people. Youngsters are drawn to his friendly face and teasing ways.

"You are a role model and a mentor," a young fan wrote to him. "You are showing us we can do anything!" said another.

Although Philip Simmons is always cheerful, he has known trouble in his long life. The great-grandson of slaves, he lived with Jim Crow laws for over fifty years. The hateful rules forced African-Americans into separate schools, hospitals, and housing. In the 1930s and 1940s, the blacksmith struggled to feed his family. This was hard to do in Charleston, where often only low-paying jobs were open to black workers.

Mr. Simmons survived the hardships and stayed with work he enjoyed. He tells young people to do the same.

"Number one, you got to love it," he says.

Philip Simmons began his career as an untrained boy. Now he is called the Dean of Blacksmiths by professional smiths across the country. His memories show that skill and patience take years of work. They also prove that everyone can achieve both. An honored artist, teacher, and businessman, Philip Simmons is the working person's hero.

Author's Note

Events in this biography are based on Philip Simmons's memories and described in his own words. He listened to the text after I wrote it. "Let me tell you the *real* story," he said if I needed to correct a detail.

When the scenes were satisfactory, the blacksmith nodded or chuckled.

"That's right, that's right," he said. "That's a true story!"

Ready to Go

Philip Simmons made up his mind. No skinny-necked egret was going to beat *him* in a staring contest. When the waterfowl threw a stony glare at him, Philip looked right back.

The bird gave in first. It tippy-toed through the silver shallows of the Wando River and fanned both wings.

"He's ready to go!" thought Philip.

The egret rose from the water, then leaned into the air. Just as quickly, it settled down in the marsh grass. Maybe the bird wasn't ready to go after all, but eight-year-old Philip was eager to leave.

Philip Simmons often uses the image of an egret in his gates.

Philip's grandmother, Sarah Buncombe Simmons, age seventy-five, circa 1920. She was of Cherokee Indian ancestry.

He waved good-bye to his grandfather and climbed in a twenty-five-foot ferry. As the boat pulled away from Daniel Island, Philip knew he "wouldn't want to turn back." Not this Saturday morning in September 1920. Not for anything.

Philip Simmons was going to Charleston for the first time in his life. Going to live with his mama, Rosa Simmons. She had worked as a housecleaner there since the age of nineteen.

Now Philip was leaving, too. Moving out of the house his grandfather built in a small farming community "up on the water." It was the only home Philip had ever known.

He was leaving his younger brother, Skeet (short for Mosquito); his little sisters, Estelle and Rosa Lee; and his grandparents, William and Sarah Simmons.

Philip clinked two quarters in his pocket. Sarah Simmons had given him the coins that morning. "Ferry costs fifteen cents for a child under twelve," she said. "Keep the rest, but don't spend it all in one place!"

Philip wiggled on his seat. Hot sunshine baked the skin under his "blouse," and he was glad he'd worn his "short-bibbed" hat. He chanted words his grandmother taught him to make time pass.

"Sing it all the way there," she told him. "Some potatoes, some potatoes, some potatoes."

Even this trick couldn't calm the boy's excited mind. He had too many questions and not enough answers.

What would the city look like? When Philip fished at the southern tip of "Dan's Island," Charleston's distant smokestacks seemed as faint as a forgotten dream.

He had heard others speak of the city's new concrete streets, but he couldn't imagine them. He knew only sandy wagon paths that cut through mossy woods like an aisle through church.

What would his new school look like? Philip would be starting second grade, but not in the one-room schoolhouse on Dan's Island. The term there lasted only three months. If the school district didn't send a teacher, Philip didn't go to school at all.

That's why Sarah Simmons insisted that he leave the island in the fall. Philip was going to Charleston to live with his mother, she told William. He was going to that brand-new public school for black children on the East Side.

Philip knew that if Sarah said "go," he'd go. If she said "come," he'd come. He was a "grandparents' boy," no doubt about it. They were strict, and he was always getting into trouble. Nothing big, but if he wandered off, they wanted to know the company he kept. Just this morning Sarah had nagged him.

"Don't get in with bad kids in Charleston!" she warned.

All the rules had made Philip "a scary one." He was a little afraid of his grandparents. Still, he worried about them. What a pile of work they had to do! Surely they couldn't get along without their oldest "grand."

Who would tote Sarah's wood every day? For years his grandmother had cooked on the stone floor of the fireplace — the same way enslaved Sea Islanders had cooked sixty years before. The family owned a wood cookstove now, but his grandmother needed someone to fire it up.

Would the food in Charleston be as tasty as Sarah's? The boy didn't think so. His favorite dish was okra soup with dried shrimp. Sarah salted fresh shrimp and put it in a paper bag until "it cure itself." When she made the soup, she poured it over rice — another custom saved from "the old memory."

Most folks in Philip's settlement picked tomatoes, peas, and corn for fifty cents a day in nearby fields. The American Fruit Growers Company owned the land and the vegetables, too. Sarah made hearty lunches for the workers, and Philip did his part.

Sea Islanders arriving in Charleston by bateau, early twentieth century

When the noon bell rang each day, he carried two buckets of hot food to the fields: "Soup on one side, rice and cornbread on the other."

Everything "on the pail" came from home. The family grew beans, corn, turnips, rutabagas, sweet potatoes, and white potatoes in their garden. Philip dug the potatoes each fall and banked them for winter meals. Who would bank the potatoes now?

As the ferry chugged past Drum Island, Charleston Harbor came into clear view. Another thought plucked the boy's mind.

What if a kid in Philip's community died? His grandfather always built the six-sided pine casket. William would need a helper to brace the boards as he cut them with a handsaw and someone to make a cedar cross for the grave.

Just as Philip commenced to brooding over dead folks, the ferry's gasoline engine slowed. The Cooper River wharves were dead ahead! The boatman guided the craft between shrimp trawlers and smaller bateaux. He cut the motor and eased the boat up to the dock.

When the ferry landed, Philip clambered out. He was happy to be off the boat. His bottom was happy too.

Philip's mother wouldn't be home from work until noon, so a neighbor was waiting for him at the house. He remembered the directions: walk two blocks up Calhoun Street and turn left on Vernon.

But what exactly was a block? Though Philip was so young that he still wore short pants, he would have to find his way around Charleston pretty fast. He heard Sarah Simmons's wise words in his head.

"There time to see and not see," she liked to say. "Time to know and not know." Philip was in the big city now. His time to see and know had finally come.

Music from the Hammer

Philip did learn his way around Charleston pretty quickly, especially the East Side. One spring day in 1923, he dawdled in front of a planter's house on Charlotte Street. Seemed like this rich man's fence called to him every afternoon when he left school. The eleven-year-old liked the bumpy layers of "Charleston Green" paint, the curve of the wiggle tails. Maybe he could sketch the wavy iron squiggles tomorrow in class.

Nineteenth-century wrought-iron fence and gate, 16 Charlotte Street, Charleston, South Carolina

Buist School didn't have a library or an auditorium. There weren't enough desks in the rooms, and seven hundred pupils crowded into the puny lunchroom every day.

Still, good-natured Philip enjoyed his school. Only two subjects could spoil his mood. English class — he hated it! And math? Well, he was sure he'd never use it anyway. He liked art, though. He was glad that some of the time, the teachers let everybody draw.

He walked east toward the Cooper River. Molten sunlight leaked from the sky and polished the water with gold. It was time to head to Washington Street, where he and his mother lived now.

Philip paused when he reached the corner of Calhoun and Washington. *Clang, bang, bang! Ping pah ping ping!* Music from a hammer grabbed him like a shark hook and pulled him toward a workshop door.

Philip forged this archway in 1986 for the Buist Academy in Charleston, South Carolina.

When he peeked inside, he went blind for a moment. The place was darker than Dan's Island at midnight. Then he saw flames. Was the shop on fire? Sparks sprayed his shirt, and he hopped backward. Wouldn't do to burn holes in his schoolclothes, wouldn't do at all.

Two "'prentice boys," or trainees, worked in the gloom. One stood by a forge — a round tub filled with dirt and fire clay. To Philip, the clay looked like cement. "The harder the fire," he noticed, "the harder he gets."

One apprentice used tongs to hold an iron rod in the forge flame. After fifteen seconds, the rod turned white-hot and sparks flew. The apprentice pulled it out of the fire and plunked it on an anvil.

Then he lifted his hammer and swung with a mighty blow — *clang!* He poured it on and poured it on, until the rod flattened out. As the rod cooled, it turned as orange as boiled shrimp.

Bang, bang! Between blows, the hammer bounced off the metal and landed on the anvil. *Ping pah ping ping!* Philip covered his ears.

"Brother, this is some action," he thought.

The apprentice was shaping an iron hinge. When the job was done, he quenched, or cooled, the metal in a bucket of water. A great sizzle of steam rose, like a spray of water against Charleston's seawall.

Another boy, Lonnie, stood next to the forge. He turned a wooden hand crank the size of a wheelbarrow wheel. Philip saw straight off that Lonnie was none too happy about his job. He grunted with every turn. Stripes of sweat ran down his face.

"I'm gonna find somethin' else to do than lift this thing," Lonnie complained. "Find something softer, lighter . . ."

Philip was curious about the strange setup. What did the crank have to do with the fire?

He heard a whinny. In the shop yard behind him, a short man was talking to a tall horse. This was the "Old Man," the master blacksmith, Peter Simmons. Philip wasn't related to Peter, but he knew him anyway. Everybody in East Charleston had heard of the fellow who could fix anything.

Blacksmith shop operated by an African-American in 1920s Charleston, South Carolina. Philip, who visited here as a boy, says it looks like Peter Simmons's shop.

Need a metal wagon tire? Go see Peter Simmons. Want to repair a stone working tool? Take it to Simmons. Horseshoes? Sure, Simmons can do the job.

Though Peter was sixty-eight years old, he looked like a boxer. Muscles braided his thick arms. His scarred hands were as tough as the leather apron that flapped around his knees.

Peter hollered to his thirteen-year-old son Lonnie. He wanted four horseshoes from the keg and the shoeing tools! Then he ordered Philip to take the horse's halter. Since Peter reminded Philip of his strict grandfather, he didn't think he should say no.

Peter Simmons at his anvil

Peter started at the kicking end of the horse. He loosened the nails on one shoe with a hammer and pulled them out with pincers. As he worked, the smith spoke softly so the animal would trust him. Philip considered the horse's point of view. Maybe a person using sharp tools on your toenail *should* feel like a friend.

Then things got interesting. The animal jerked his head and stomped his feet, just like a pouty child. Philip enjoyed watching the horse "kicking up," but Peter moved back a little farther.

"Put the twister on him!" he ordered.

"OK, Mr. Peter," Philip said. "I can do that." Philip wedged a stick in the animal's mouth and twisted the rope tied to the stick. The twister made the horse so uncomfortable that it forgot to kick.

After paring all four hooves, Peter let each new shoe "fry" in the forge. Then he "foot it," or measured it to the hoof. He hammered the shoe on, angling the nails down, out, and away from the quick.

"Boy, don't you ever drive that nail into the nerve," Peter warned Philip. "You hit her wrong, she'll kick you over the moon!"

Holding a balky horse was hard, but Philip wanted to see if he could do it. Besides, he liked the action. He also enjoyed the couple of pennies that Peter gave him. Maybe he could try his hand at the forge next time. Make his own sparks fly and "get big arms," just like Old Man Simmons.

A Lot of Story

In 1924 Philip Simmons needed more than big arms. He needed money, plain and simple.

Yesterday he bought newspapers, two for a nickel, and hawked them on the corner for five cents each. This morning he polished shoes for a regular customer at the corner of Calhoun and Alexander and earned a nickel plus tip. Yet it wasn't enough. It was never enough.

What could a twelve-year-old boy with empty pockets do on a wintry Saturday? No use going to the diamond. Baseball season was over. Should he visit the shoemaker's shop? Nope, things were too quiet there. Maybe he would wander over to Number Four Calhoun.

There were fifteen blacksmith shops on the Charleston peninsula. Sometimes the boy crossed Calhoun to watch Ducky Logan at his forge or he visited David Kidd's shop over by the big market.

Philip liked Peter's place the best. The Old Man still wouldn't let him near the forge. "Too dangerous," Mr. Peter said. But Philip knew where the broom was kept. He could sweep up the iron slivers that fell from the anvil and make "a few pennies, maybe a quarter."

When Philip reached the shop door, he could barely squeeze inside. He was used to seeing folks in Mr. Peter's place. The Old Man had "a lot of story" to pass on and "did more for the talking than anyone."

Still, the boy had never seen a crowd like this. Farmers and city folks. Grown-ups and kids. All gathered around Peter's anvil as if watching a dogfight.

The master smith was making a metal wagon tire from a 2 ½ -by- ⅜ -inch rod. Lonnie and a new apprentice boy — Peter wore out his helpers pretty fast — were the strikers. They stood behind the anvil holding eight-pound sledgehammers. Between them stood Peter with a smaller ball peen.

The Old Man knew exactly where the sledgehammers should land. When the rod turned white-hot, he pulled it out of the fire and set it on the anvil. Overlapping the ends, he tapped the joint — here, there, here — with his hammer.

After each tap, the strikers swung. What a sight! Arms falling. Hammers zinging. Sparks flying as the apprentices welded "unruly" metal into metal. It was loud, sweaty, fast work. And it was the most "action" Philip had ever seen in one place.

While they pounded, Peter whistled the rhythm of the hammers: "Toot-do-do, toot, toot." The crowd loved it. They buzzed with questions.

"Peter, what you doin'?" one fellow called. "How could you work with people talking to you?"

"I don't work with my mouth, I work with my hand," the master smith bragged.

When the metal cooled, Peter put it back in the fire for another heat. After three heats and thirty blows, he hit the anvil with the side of his hammer. This was his signal for the strikers to stop. Like John Henry on the railroad, each one threw his sledgehammer down.

Lonnie's arm looked ready to break. His mother claimed Peter was working him too hard. "You gonna kill that boy," she told her husband.

Philip felt bad for Lonnie, but he had to smile. There was no better showman than Peter Simmons. No better worker, either. From Peter's stories, Philip knew the master smith had learned about work the hard way.

Peter was born into slavery in 1855. His father, Guy Simmons, was an enslaved plantation blacksmith. As a boy, Peter studied ironworking with his daddy.

Guy was a tough old bird who could swing two sledgehammers at once. Peter tried not to get on his father's wrong side. If he made a mistake at the forge, Guy would "clip" him on the shoulder with the back of a hammer.

After Peter grew up and opened his own shop in 1890, he worked the tar out of his own helpers. Yet he never hit them. From what Philip had seen, the master was a patient teacher. When an apprentice made a mistake, Peter stopped and explained things right away.

Peter Simmons with his nephew and apprentice, Robert Simmons

Philip watched as Peter's helpers rolled the tire in a trench and poured on a can of water to "cool him off."

"Maybe it's time for me to put down the shoeshine box, and the newspaper, put it down, too," Philip thought. "Do wagon wheels and horseshoes instead of people's shoes."

"Let me go to work for you," Philip begged Mr. Peter, but the Old Man wasn't too crazy about the idea. "When you get to be thirteen," he said, "come back and see me."

So Philip "started counting the hours and the minutes." Though Mr. Peter was smart, there was one thing he didn't know: if you're twelve years old, thirteen seems a long way down the road.

Every Tool to Every Work

M oney problems can upset your mind, but a mosquito will worry you to death. Philip chased the "skeeter" away from his neck. There were plenty of other kids in his sixth-grade class this late spring morning in 1925. Let the rascal light on somebody else.

Plus, it was cooking in here! Long pants made Philip's legs feel like fried sausages. To keep his mind off the heat, he considered the vacation months ahead.

"In sixty-two years," Philip says, "I never went in the shop and didn't need a hammer."

In a few weeks, he would take the ferry to Daniel Island and help his grandparents on the farm, just as he did each year. But this would have to be his last summer on the island. Skeet and Estelle were living in Charleston now, too. Philip was their "Big Bubba." There was no one else to help support them and his mother, Rosa.

Philip yanked at the mosquito and squashed it in his palm. He needed to earn money. Somehow, some way. Come September, he would be thirteen years and three months old. Mr. Peter would have to let him work then.

By fall Peter was ready to hire Philip except for one thing. "You can't go full-time," he cautioned the boy. "Not until you're fifteen."

So Philip agreed to work each day after school. And that's when Peter "got excited" about Philip, and Philip "got excited" about him. Especially when Peter said he would earn a dollar and a half a week. Now the boy could see ironworking "in that shop, on that anvil, by *him,*" the master teacher.

The new apprentice "got a lot of school" at Number Four Calhoun. For five months, Peter taught him the names of fifty tools and their proper place in the shop. "Every tool to every work," Philip learned.

But when Philip found out about the crank, he wished he'd never asked. A belt connected the crank to a leather lung called a bellows, and a pipe connected the bellows to the forge. Every time Philip turned the crank, the bellows blew air into the pipe. The stream of oxygen kept the fire at about 2,300 degrees Fahrenheit.

Philip hated the bellows as much as Lonnie did. The awkward thing was touchier than a thirteen-year-old boy. Sometimes gas collected inside the big lung. When the gas exploded, the blast forced too much air into the forge and put the flame out.

Peter showed his apprentice how to burn wood down to red coals and when to add the "original blacksmith coal." The harder coal kept the fire from burning too hot or fast.

To "catch the fire and keep it going," Philip wet the coals. Then he raked them away from the air hole in the center of the forge. Clinkers, or chunks of waste metal, had to be scraped away, too.

The master finally let Philip take a lick with the sledgehammer. Philip "tried and

Tools in Philip Simmons's blacksmith shop, Charleston, South Carolina

tried to get big arms," but the heavy tool wore him out. Peter showed him a better way.

"You just lift the hammer, boy," Peter explained. "It'll carry itself down."

The hard work paid off when Peter gave Philip and Lonnie a small job to do on their own. This was a test of skill for the boys. As they set to work on a broken push-cart, Philip was thankful his grandfather had taught him carpentry. He and Lonnie had to "get the wheel off the wheelbarrow, put it on the side, and make the wagon."

A small job meant small pay. Maybe a watermelon or some sugarcane. That was fine with Philip. He liked the chance to prove himself.

The Old Man trained eight men and ten boys in all. None worked as hard as Philip.

When five o'clock rolled around, the other helpers called it quits. Not Philip Simmons. Though he was "glad to see that evening shadow," he stuck it out to sundown.

Lonnie finally got sick of the trade. He left Charleston to play saxophone for a jazz band in the North. But blacksmithing agreed with Philip, and he quit school at fifteen to work full-time.

After a few more years in the shop, he "felt proud" that he "could do a lot of things" on his own. Best of all, once a year, Peter gave him a dollar-a-week raise. Then suddenly everything changed. And Philip found out that life could be like a bellows sometimes. When you least expected it, it sure could backfire.

Lever-operated bellows forces air through the chimney and into a forge on the other side.
Museum of American Frontier Culture, Staunton, Virginia

Father of All Trades

One summer day in 1928, sixteen-year-old Philip was working outside. He was wondering why there were fewer customers than usual when a crazy-looking wagon drove by.

Hold on! The rear platform looked familiar. The wooden wheels were the same. But if this was a wagon, where was the horse? Instead of reins, the driver clutched a tall steering wheel.

Philip was used to automobiles. When he first moved to Charleston, one or two horseless carriages passed through town every month. And these days cars were as common as Charleston rats. Few merchants in the city owned a truck, though.

The driver called to Philip.

"What you gonna do?" the fellow asked. "Mr. Thomas, Mr. Howard on East Bay Street, he buying *trucks*! Won't be any more horses to shoe, wagons to repair. You in trouble!"

So this was why business had slowed down!

Peter Simmons was inside at the forge. He overheard the conversation and called to Philip.

"Come here, boy," he ordered. "Don't you listen to what that guy's telling you about blacksmithing being a 'lost art.'"

"But we're not getting the amount of work like we used to," Philip argued.

"There's always gonna be something for the blacksmith to do," Peter said.

What if Peter was wrong? All that training. And for what? No money. No future. Nothing but a truck rumbling down Calhoun Street, passing the blacksmith by.

Truck in front of blacksmith shop, circa 1918

But Peter was right. A week later, the same driver was back and looking a little foolish. His truck frame needed pockets for tall metal stakes. These would keep a load from falling off the bed.

Installing the stakes was easy enough. It was the "same principle, same identical thing" as fixing a wagon. And it was a kissing cousin to toolmaking and horseshoeing. Blacksmithing, Philip decided, was "the father of all trades," including bodywork.

Two years later, another truck stopped in front of the shop. Eighteen-year-old Philip slipped on his cap and stepped outside. It was still early in the day. A hard wind blew diamonds of light across the river. Overhead, a hungry seagull screamed like a rusty hinge.

This vehicle was from the Johnson Coal Yard, the one near the fish dock. The driver unloaded huge metal coal buckets — "big buckets hold about a ton and a half."

Schooners with a load of coal often sailed into Charleston Harbor. Cranes hoisted tubs of coal from the ship to the dock. If a tub swung into the wharf, the metal tore.

Now three tubs needed repair, but Philip felt strange doing the big job alone. Seventy-six-year-old Peter was in the hospital for surgery. He had left his best apprentice in charge.

Philip was concerned about the Old Man. Peter was like a father to him. It was Peter who had raised his salary to four dollars a week, Peter who had closed down the shop to watch him play left field for the Diamond Sluggers baseball team, Peter who predicted that blacksmiths would survive.

Philip eyeballed the large job in front of him. Could he pass this test, too? Well, he had learned to "feel his ability" in the shop. He would "cut the patch out and put hole in it and rivet it together."

The apprentice punched holes in the tub and matched them with holes in the patch. After heating a rivet, or short piece of metal, he pounded it through the holes. The shaft of the rivet swelled and held the joint tight. Then Philip flattened the rivet on both sides with a hammer.

The young smith discovered that being in charge was no "horseshoe show." Those patches needed more rivets than a squash has seeds! The job took him a week to finish.

As he wrote the bill, he wished he had "loved math more" in school. To figure the charge, he added the total hours worked, multiplied them by his hourly fee, and included the cost of the iron.

Philip carried the bill to the Johnson Coal Yard himself. Though the walk to the fish dock was a short one, it changed him for good. When he left the shop, he was still a "'prentice boy." When he returned with a check for $35, he was a businessman.

Anxious to share his big news, Philip visited Peter in Roper Hospital, a separate building for black patients at the all-white Memorial Hospital.

"That's what I would have done," the master smith said about Philip's repair, "and that's what I would have charged them."

Mr. Peter signed the check and told Philip he could keep half of the money. The apprentice was amazed. From a measly salary of $4 last week to $17.50 this week! It was more than he had ever made at one time in his life.

"Philip," he said to himself, "this is the right thing for you. Money's in it!"

Now that he was a fifty-fifty partner, Philip felt like a master craftsman. After that day, everything he put his hands on "just fall in place" and "seemed like gold." Especially when he met a "quiet-going" young woman named Erthaline Porchie.

The Boss

Philip's mother, the hard-working Rosa, died of a heart attack at home in 1932. Saddened by her death, Philip needed someone to cheer him up. Ertha Porchie (pronounced "Pore-SHAY") was a pretty girl with skin as soft as a Low Country breeze. She was so shy that she never liked to have her photograph made.

Maybe she was *too* quiet. Would she even have "enough nerve to sit down and entertain" him, Philip wondered. When he found that she had a "sly" flirty way about her too, he was pleased.

If you admire someone the way Philip admired Ertha, there's only one thing to do.

"Every spear is different," Philip Simmons says.

Marry her. Philip wed his girlfriend in 1936. He was twenty-four, and she was seventeen.

Around the same time, Peter Simmons moved across the Cooper River to run a smaller shop. He gave Philip the Calhoun Street place as a wedding gift. Now Philip was a master craftsman, a husband, and the boss of his own shop.

But Philip worried about his old friend.

"You got to remember where you come from," the young smith reminded himself.

Once a week, after working until four P.M., he crossed the river by ferry and gave the eighty-year-old blacksmith "a good three, three and a half hours" of help at the forge.

As Philip fathered Peter, he raised his own children, too. In four years, he and Ertha had two daughters and a son. To support them, Philip needed every blacksmithing job he could find. Since these were the Depression years, folks were short of money. Times were hard, and Philip struggled to stay in business.

Then one day in 1938, a man visited Philip's shop. "Mr. Simmons," the fellow said, "I got a broken piece in my gate. Could you repair it?"

City homeowners were fixing up their iron gates and fences. Many of the ornamental pieces were one or two centuries old. Some were made by white smiths. Some may have been made by African-American smiths: men like Guilom in 1700; Cuffee in 1739; Benya in 1786; Toby Richardson in 1850.

But no one forged new pieces now. Who could restore the old ones? There was only one thing to do. Call on the best blacksmith in town.

Philip grabbed his hand drill and a rivet. He trotted over to the house and riveted a broken scroll into the gate. The job was no different from fixing wagons or trucks. As usual, he did the work with pride.

When word spread about Philip's careful repair, other jobs came his way. Fixing the gates gave him an idea.

"My family has to eat," he thought. "I got the forge, and I [can] turn 'em out like the old original."

In a short time, Philip was forging new gates with the old-fashioned patterns he studied as a boy: snaky wiggle tails, S-shaped scrolls, spear-topped bars.

Each gate began as a sketch. In an instant, Philip could tell if the bars were too

Hammer Gate, 254 Coming Street, Charleston, South Carolina

close together. He could judge if a scroll had too much "belly" or needed more open space. His designs were perfectly balanced. Like notes in a song, each part harmonized with the other.

Making gates excited the blacksmith's imagination. He thought about the natural beauty of the Low Country — "the fish in the sea, the tree in the woods, a flower in the garden." When he added these images to his designs, iron tulips, magnolias, and pecan leaves began to bloom all over Charleston. Now Philip Simmons was an artist, though he didn't call himself one.

Sometimes a client brought Philip a sketch. "To catch the picture of what they wanted," Philip had to "read the customer's mind." That was fine with the blacksmith. "A satisfied customer," he believed, "is an advertising customer."

One woman wanted an iron wheelbarrow at the end of her porch railing. "OK," Philip said, "I can make it for you." When a customer asked for thirty-six oyster knives, Philip obliged.

The smith loved his customers and liked to please them. One time an upholsterer made a strange request. He wanted a three-panel gate, and he wanted wooden tack hammers inserted in the center of each one.

Philip knew the wooden hammers would rot. So he forged three life-sized hammers from iron, cut openings in the bars of the gate, and welded the tools in place.

The blacksmith liked to tease his customers, too.

"Upholstery man, I put a hammer," he said. "But you, the plumber," he told a plumber, "I put a toilet bowl!"

If there's a gate in Charleston with "Japanese plum" tree leaves, watch out. Plum wine is "twelve to fifteen percent alcohol." Might be a bootlegger living in that house!

Philip has designed three heart gates for the Philip Simmons Garden, St. John's
Reformed Episcopal Church, Charleston, South Carolina.

Work with What You Have

The 1930s were good years for Philip. Then life backfired again in 1940. Ertha became so sick that she entered Roper Hospital. After six weeks of daily visits from her husband, she seemed better.

But one morning even Philip couldn't make her well. She died on the afternoon of August 12, 1940. Though Philip was shocked, he kept his grief inside. It was *"very hard"* for him to talk about Ertha. He couldn't even bring himself to look at her death certificate.

She was *"so young"* when she passed! To ease his mind, he tried smoking and drinking. The whiskey burned his throat, and he couldn't inhale smoke. All he could do with cigarettes was hold them between his lips and "wet 'em down." One day he realized he was setting "a bad example." He couldn't afford such foolishness, not with three kids to raise.

"You take what God gives you," Philip said, "and work with what you have." His children were toddlers, ages one to four. They needed a mother, he decided. He placed them with caring kinfolk and friends on the East Side. This way he could visit the kids and earn a living for them, too.

Philip kept "busy, busy, busy." He became more active in St. John's Reformed Episcopal Church. He worked with the YMCA and the Boy Scouts, and he played more baseball. The Diamond Sluggers were one of six teams in the local Pony League. The men didn't travel, but they wore snappy blue and gray uniforms. And they were good enough to play the Negro League teams that passed through town.

Thirty-year-old Philip was a strong, gentle fellow. Women liked the widower, and some tried to "hook" him. One wanted to marry him. Philip thought it over. The kids were settled into new homes with new mothers. No use upsetting them. Besides, he was too busy to get lonesome.

But he was stumped. How would he save the lady's feelings? Then it came to him — he would introduce her to a friend of his. The experiment was a success. She fell in love with the guy, married him, and everyone was content. And just as the "crick" flows into the ocean, Philip's years as a bachelor rolled steadily on.

The Old Ways

Y ou must be Philip Simmons," the young man said. Sixty-year-old Philip looked up from his pile of scrap iron. The year was 1972, and he was working in his shop yard on Blake Street. Philip shook the visitor's hand. Who was this fellow, anyway? He said he was a graduate student from Indiana, but he had Washington, D.C., plates on his car.

Was he lost? Well, yes, he was. John Michael Vlach had been wandering around the one-way streets near Philip's shop, looking for the man who knew "the old ways of

Wiggle tail, 2 Stoll's Alley, Charleston, South Carolina. The round bumps are rivets.

ironwork." John seemed a little nervous, maybe because a scruffy dog named Brownie was barking at him. But the blacksmith liked to talk about old times, so the scholar soon relaxed.

Philip explained the history of his business to John. In the late 1930s, the federal government gave Charleston enough money to build two East Side housing projects: one for black citizens and one for whites. So Philip had to move his shop "for the improvement of the city."

The smith moved four times and landed on Blake Street in 1969. It was here that he replaced the spiteful bellows with an electric forge blower.

By the time America entered World War II in 1941, most of the city's blacksmiths were gone. When the Charleston Naval Ship Yard wanted parts for ships, they went to Philip Simmons. But after the war was over in 1945, business slowed down.

"I needed to make some money on the side," Philip told John. He drove a taxi, ran a dry-cleaning business, and opened and closed a restaurant. There must be a faster way to "grab a few more pennies," he thought.

Peter Simmons had died in 1953, two days before his ninety-eighth birthday. About this time, Philip decided to modernize his own shop. He bought an electric arc welder that was three times faster than riveting. And he attached an old washing machine motor to his hand drill. Both tools speeded up the work.

When John Vlach wanted to compare the old ways to the new ones, Philip took him on a tour of Charleston. He led John down a narrow alley to one of his first "fancy" pieces. Philip was proud of the old-time rivets he had used to join the wiggle tail to the gate.

Next, the two men looked at a bird gate. The customer had given Philip a drawing of an egret. "Can you make it?" the fellow had asked.

Sure he could. Philip knew egrets like the calluses on his hands. He used an acetylene torch to cut the metal talons, and he made a bended knee so the bird was "looking ready to go."

Philip drove John over to East Bay Street to see his Snake Gate. It took him one month to forge that gate. He thought he'd never finish the eye. At first, it stared as if it

Egret Gate, 2 St. Michael's Alley, Charleston, South Carolina

Overthrow of Snake Gate, 329 East Bay Street, Charleston, South Carolina

were dead. Philip "heat and beat, heat and beat, heat and beat," until the snake looked as real as a diamond head rattler. "If it bites you," Philip joked, "you better get to the doctor fast. Blood get up to your heart, you know what happens!"

John Vlach was impressed. These were no ordinary pieces of ornamental iron-work. They were sculpture! Philip Simmons was not just a blacksmith. He was an artist.

John saw Philip often over the next four years. He helped install gates, took pho-tographs, and tape-recorded conversations. And in 1976, John offered Philip the great-est test of his career: an invitation to make a gate at the Festival of American Folklife, a summer-long event in Washington, D.C.

The two men discussed the trip in the dim light of Philip's shop. As they spoke, pinpoints of sun poked through the sheet metal walls. At first the artist didn't want to go.

"No, no, no, no, no," Philip said. He held two scrolls up to the light to see if they matched. "I got business to do."

This wasn't going to be easy. John raked his hands through his dark brown hair. "You'll only be gone fifteen days," he said.

"Any special piece that you want me to make?" Philip asked.

"The choice is yours," John sweet-talked him. "We just want you to come up and demonstrate what you're doing in Charleston."

This offer made sense to the businessman. He could make something small to bring home and "sell for a profit."

"What about the materials? How will I move them?"

"We'll put everything in the trunk of your car."

"Only so much I can do without my 'prentice boys."

"Bring the apprentices with you. We'll pay their expenses, and they can drive the car."

The blacksmith ran out of arguments. "Yes, I'll come," he finally agreed.

There were a few other hurdles. First, Philip needed a portable forge. He always "liked to make the odd thing," so he cut the top off an old hot water heater and packed it with fire clay. He

The personalized gate features the owner's initials.

Philip Simmons forges a scroll in the early 1970s.

didn't spend more than fifty dollars on his homemade invention.

Second, what kind of gate should he make? Philip "set to the desk," but nothing came to mind. He lay awake at night. Still no ideas. Six weeks passed. Suddenly he realized he was leaving — tomorrow!

Would this be the first test the blacksmith failed? When the airplane left Charleston the next day, Philip peeked out the small oval window next to his seat. He took a long look at the rivers and marshes that hugged Charleston on three sides.

"I'm just crazy about the water," he thought. "Maybe I'll show the stars in the water."

He considered fish. "Fish represents Charleston. It's known for fishing."

Philip imagined the moon over the Cooper River and decided to show a "quarter-moon, just racing along."

But like the old Sea Island tale says, "'sidering and 'cidering won't buy Sal a new shirt." The artist pulled out a scrap of paper and began to draw. By the time the plane landed an hour later, he had solved the puzzle.

He would make a fish in the water and a double star in the sky, one inside the other. "Like watchin' a star," he thought, "it get smaller on you." Two quarter-moons would shine over it all.

Maybe this wouldn't be his prettiest gate, but it would be his most important one. It would be his "sacrificial piece." The one made in front of thousands of people and forged with the ancient tools of ironworking: fire, hammer, and a blacksmith's rugged hands.

The Festival

Washington, D.C., was almost as hot as Charleston. Especially the last week of July and first week of August 1976. For these two weeks, Philip and his apprentices, Joseph Pringle and Silas Sessions, worked on the grassy Mall near the Lincoln Memorial. When the sun grew too bright, they moved under a striped tent.

The United States was two hundred years old, and the festival was a birthday party. It celebrated the skills of people from all over the world. Philip was impressed with the other talented folks he saw on the Mall: singers, dancers, cooks, hairdressers, gospel singers, woodcarvers, and seamstresses.

"Everybody on this ground," he noticed, "is doing it the old way."

At first, he and his helpers forged simple chandeliers and plant stands. The rain of sparks and ring of hammers drew a stream of visitors to the demonstration. Philip answered their questions, just as Peter Simmons had done fifty years before.

Then the blacksmiths began the Star and Fish Gate. They cut lengths of iron bars, forged pecan leaves, welded J-curves inside of S-curves. Philip used several pieces of metal to create an open effect in the spot-tailed bass. Finally he made the striking star within a star.

Toward the end of Philip's stay in Washington, John noticed something curious about the outside star.

"The center point is off by twenty degrees," he commented.

"A star can shine all different ways," the artist explained.

That evening Philip started thinking. Nothing is right until it's right. His grandfather had taught him that as a boy on Daniel Island. Peter Simmons had drilled it into

Star and Fish Gate, 1976

Detail of Star and Fish Gate

him as a young man. And what about his customers? "If it weren't for them," Philip thought, "I wouldn't even be in Washington."

The blacksmith tossed all night in his dormitory bed at George Washington University. The next day, he hurried to the Mall before anyone else was around. It took him fifteen minutes to cut the star out of the gate and weld it back in place.

By the time the demonstrations began at eleven A.M., the star pointed straight up toward the enamel blue sky. Philip Simmons had proved himself once more. And though he didn't know it yet, he had hooked his future to that star.

Afterword

The Star and Fish Gate sparked a national interest in Philip Simmons's work. Festival officials invited him again in 1977, and in 1981 John Michael Vlach published *Philip Simmons, Charleston Blacksmith*. That year John suggested his friend's name for a Heritage Fellowship. The federal government gives this award to artists who are considered "national treasures."

Philip Simmons was one of "fifteen head" of people who won. He returned to Washington in 1982 to accept the award and to join the festival again. The same year, the Smithsonian Institution bought his Star and Fish Gate. Now it's a national piece that travels to museums around the country.

State awards followed. In 1988 the blacksmith won a South Carolina Folk Heritage Award. He was admitted into the South Carolina State Hall of Fame in 1994.

The city of Charleston was the last to "get on the bandwagon." Some say this is because Charlestonians take African-American craftsmen for granted. Local officials finally followed the example of state and national agencies. In 1995 they gave Mr. Simmons a Conservation Craftsman Award.

Every year, more tributes come the blacksmith's way. He doesn't dwell on the success. Instead, like Peter Simmons, he concentrates on his role as a teacher.

Since 1955, Philip Simmons has taught at least five apprentices. Two of them, Joseph Pringle, a cousin, and Carlton Simmons, a nephew, are now fully trained smiths. Both are the latest in a long line of African-American blacksmiths in Charleston.

The silver-headed Mr. Simmons puts it this way: "I say to people, 'There won't be another Philip, but there will be another Joseph or Carlton.'"

Like generations of blacksmiths before him, Mr. Simmons has passed on the tradition. And now the Historic Charleston Foundation plans to open a Philip Simmons training center for young blacksmiths. The center will grant the artist his deepest wish: "to teach more kids."

"You got to teach kids while the sap is young," he believes, "just like you got to beat the iron while it's hot."

With such devotion to community, the blacksmith might seem like "Saint Philip." Those who are close to him know he can be a trickster, too. He likes riddles, and he never takes himself too seriously.

"Some people are so heavenly bound," he jokes, "that they do no earthly good."

Even the heavy mantle of racism seems to sit lightly on his shoulders. Despite Charleston's history of slavery and segregation, Mr. Simmons and his white customers have a mutual respect for one another. He does have some gentle advice on race, however.

"When you start talking about color," he suggests, "be particular, because color's important."

A graceful man with mahogany brown skin, Mr. Simmons uses a can of green paint to make his point. "There's dark green, light green, black, and white in that paint," he says. "We should get together and enjoy everybody's color."

The artist is loyal to his East Charleston neighborhood, where he lives in a small cottage. "Look at all I have," he says of his simple house and the family and friends who visit every day. "I have everything I need."

Yet there are few luxuries in his life, and some people think he undercharges for his designs. "I don't have too much money," he admits, "but I got a pretty good reputation."

Philip Simmons has far more than that. From "horse buggy wheels to carts, carriages, wagons, trucks, and gates," he learned to change with the times. No matter the task, he has brought pride and honor to every job. Perhaps he knows the secret to true wealth: never give up the work you love.

"Money will come if you love it," he says. "It's like baseball or football. You play it because you love it."

Notes and Bibliography

I visited Philip Simmons on March 5, 1992; December 12, 1995; and May 4–11, 1996. Most quotations are from these visits or from telephone conversations with him on June 15 and June 23, 1996.

On June 3, 1996, John Vlach shared his memories of meeting Philip Simmons for the first time. On June 7, he recalled the story of Philip changing the star in the gate.

John Vlach's biography of Philip Simmons provided other quotations and most of the background information. Vlach's respect for Philip Simmons and his art shines on every page of *Charleston Blacksmith: The Work of Philip Simmons.* Athens: University of Georgia Press, 1981. Reprint. Columbia: University of South Carolina Press, 1992.

Other quotations were gathered from these sources:

Brazell, Dawn. "Philip Simmons: Love of Craft Stokes Artist's Enthusiasm." *The* [Charleston, South Carolina] *News and Courier,* February 22, 1992, sec. F: 1, 3.

Flanders, Danny. "Forging Ahead." *The* [Columbia, South Carolina] *State,* June 9, 1996, "Home" sec.: 4–6.

Keeper of the Gate. Documentary film. Charleston, S.C.: The Philip Simmons Foundation, 1994.

Perkins, Otis. "Blacksmith Loves His Ancient Art." *The* [Charleston, South Carolina] *News and Courier,* November 19, 1957, sec. A: 3.

Philip Simmons, Blacksmith. Documentary film. Columbia: South Carolina Arts Commission, 1976.

"Retired Negro Blacksmith Dies in Mt. Pleasant at 97." Undated clipping in "Philip Simmons" file, Avery Research Center for African-American History and Culture, College of Charleston, Charleston, S.C.

Rogers, Alan. *Forge & Anvil.* Instructional film series, segment on Philip Simmons. Athens: University of Georgia, 1995.

Student letters to Philip Simmons. December 1, 1995. Cainhoy School, Huger, S.C.

Vlach, John Michael. "The Craftsman and the Communal Image: Philip Simmons, Charleston Blacksmith." *Family Heritage,* 1979, vol. 2: 14–19.

——. "Philip Simmons: Afro-American Blacksmith." *Black People and Their Culture.* Ed. Linn Shapiro. Washington, D.C.: Smithsonian Institution, 1976, 35–37.

Historical background on Charleston was gathered from these sources:

Fraser, Edward J. *Charleston! Charleston!* Columbia: University of South Carolina Press, 1989.

"Historical Sketch of Buist School, 1920–1954." Charleston, S.C.: Buist School, March 21, 1954.

"MESDA Craftsmen." (Computer printout of African-American craftsmen in the South before 1820.) Winston-Salem, N.C.: Museum of Early Southern Decorative Arts, 1990.

Student from Buist Academy on Visitor's Center Gate, Charleston, South Carolina

Books of Interest

Branch, Muriel Miller. *The Water Brought Us: The Story of the Gullah-Speaking People.* New York: Cobblehill, 1995.

Carawan, Guy, and Candie. *Ain't You Got a Right to the Tree of Life?* New York: Simon and Schuster, 1966. Reprint. Athens: University of Georgia Press, 1989.

Daise, Ronald. *Reminiscences of Sea Island Heritage.* Orangeburg, S.C.: Sandlapper Publishing, 1986.

Family Across the Sea. Documentary film. Columbia: South Carolina Educational Television Network, 1989.

Krull, Kathleen. *Bridges to Change: How Kids Live on a South Carolina Sea Island.* New York: Lodestar, 1995.

Lyons, Mary E., comp. *Raw Head, Bloody Bones: African-American Tales of the Supernatural.* New York: Scribner, 1991. Paper edition. New York: Simon and Schuster, 1994.

Watson, Aldren A. *The Village Blacksmith.* New York: Crowell, 1968.

Philip Simmons's works are in these museums: Museum of International Folk Art, Santa Fe, New Mexico: *Window Grille;* Museum of American History, Smithsonian Institution, Washington, D.C.: *The Star and Fish Gate;* South Carolina State Museum, Columbia, South Carolina: *The Philip Simmons Gate;* Atlanta History Center: *Olympic-theme Gate*

Peter Simmons's anvil is over one hundred years old. It is displayed at the Avery Research Center for African-American History and Culture, College of Charleston, Charleston, South Carolina.

For other color photographs of Philip Simmons's works, see:

Uncommon Beauty in Common Objects: The Legacy of African American Craft Art. Ed. Barbara Glass. Wilberforce, Ohio: National Afro-American Museum and Cultural Center, 1993, p. 92.

Shaw, Robert. *America's Traditional Crafts.* [New York:] Hugh Lauter Levin Associates, 1993, pp. 290–292.

Siporin, Steve. *American Folk Masters: The National Heritage Fellows.* New York: Harry N. Abrams, 1992.

Acknowledgments

For their generous help in Charleston, I thank Mannie Garcia; Stephen Hoffius of the South Carolina Historical Society; Bill and Carolyn Michaels; Bishop James West and the congregation of St. John's Reformed Episcopal Church; Aubrey, Carl, Crystal, and David from Buist Academy; and the Philip Simmons Foundation, P.O. Box 21585, Charleston, South Carolina 29413-1585.

In Charlottesville, Virginia, thanks to my husband, Paul Collinge; Ann J. Smith; Dale Morse, Susan Bloom, and Steve Stokes of Stokes of England Blacksmith Shop; and Emily Behler and Jean Majeski of the Village School. I am also grateful to David McCullough and Joy Hakim, who shared their lively and inspiring works of nonfiction at the 1996 Virginia Festival of the Book.

Deepest thanks to John Michael Vlach, who shared his scholarship, photographs, and memories. Finally, thank you, Mr. Simmons, for your wit, wisdom, and marvelous stories. They are a gift to the world.

Philip Simmons, 1996

Index

Page numbers appearing in bold type refer to pages that contain photographs.

DATE DUE

AG3 0 99			
JUL 2 5 2007			
AUG 2 3 2010			
DEC 27 2011			

GAYLORD | | | PRINTED IN U.S.A.